PARENT'S LITTLE BOOK OF WISDOM

A Couple Hundred Suggestions, Observations and Reminders for Parents to Read, Remember and Share.

By Buck Tilton & Melissa Gray

ICS BOOKS, Inc.
Merrillville, IN

Parent's Little Book of Wisdom

Copyright © 1996 by Buck Tilton & Melissa Gray

10 9 8 7 6 5 4 3 2 1

All rights reserved, including the right to reproduce this book or portions thereof
in any form or by any means, electronic or mechanical, including photocopying,
recording, unless authorization is obtained, in writing, from the publisher.
All inquiries should be addressed to ICS Books, Inc, 1370 E. 86th Place, Merrillville, IN 46410

Published by:
ICS BOOKS, Inc
1370 E. 86th Place
Merrillville, IN 46410
800-541-7323

Co-Published in Canada by:
Vanwell Publishing LTD
1 Northrup Crescent
St. Catharines, Ontario
L2M 6P5
800-661-6136

Printed in the U.S.A.
All ICS titles are printed on 50% recycled paper fro
pre-consumer waste. All sheets are processed witho
using acid.

Library of Congress Cataloging-in-Publication Data

Due to government shutdown, no CIP information was available at press time.
Please call ICS BOOKS and we will be glad to fax over CIP information when available.
Call toll free 800-541-7323

Dedication

For Amber Leah and
McKenzie Erin and
Zachary Gray.

Preface

"Knowledge is the parent of love; wisdom, itself."
– Julius Charles Hare and Augustus William Hare.

When we started collecting the thoughts that would eventually become this little book, we realized, almost from the beginning, that much of what we consider "wisdom for parents" overlaps into every area of life. And so it should be. One who is wise in the ways of parenting is, of course, wise in the ways of living. When you cultivate yourself as a parent, you cultivate yourself as a whole person.

Nothing here is original because nothing about parenting is original. Many of these words are our own, some are adapted and some borrowed, but all of these thoughts have been around, in essence, since the first mom and dad watched the first baby sleeping and said, "How can we do the best job possible?" We hope you hold this book because you ask yourself the same question.

There is no pretense here, either. We goof up as often as anybody else, and every day vow to be better the next. That, too, is as it should be. The birth of a child does not make a person a parent. It is a process that will be full of joy and sorrow, a journey full of wonder and worry.

For what it's worth, this is the partial sharing of a journey, not a source of wisdom. There is no intention of telling you how to raise your children. Awareness is the greatest virtue of the wise, and if this book stimulates you to become a little more aware as a parent, we will consider our time more than well spent. If you turn away from these words and tune in consciously to your own heart, you will find the source of wisdom. Farewell.

Buck Tilton and Melissa Gray

1. Love your children simply
    because they were born.

2. No one said it would be easy being a parent.

3. Someone should have said it would be easy.

4. You never get a second chance to make a first impression every day on your child.

5. Do not let the tyranny of the urgent take precedence over the urgency of the important.

6. Do the important today. When today is gone, it is gone forever.

7.   Quality is more important than quantity.

8.   Sometimes your child needs quantity, too.

9. You will enjoy least in your child those things you enjoy least in yourself.

10. You are defined by your actions, not your words.

11. Your child will always hear more than you say.

12. Do not expect respect from a child who receives none.

13. Do not expect love from a child who receives none.

14. Love without expectations.

15. "Preconceived notions are the locks on the door to wisdom."

– Merry Browne.

16. Using force on a child will not gain worthy results.

17. Do not discourage curiosity. It is the
root of knowledge.

18. Do not discourage initiative. It is the
root of intelligence.

19. Do not discourage individuality. It is the
root of wisdom.

20. Nature's course is perfect. Allow your child to follow it.

21. Campfires create a circle of warmth and light that bind a family together for much longer than the wood burns.

22. Love yourself. It is perhaps the greatest example you can set.

23. Love your partner. It is perhaps the second greatest example you can set.

24. Your child will want to be like you whether you love yourself and your partner or not.

25. Negativity breeds negativity.

26. Unlimited is the suffering of an unpraised child.

27. Spend less time teaching to and more time learning from your child.

28. There is more love in a hug than in all the words ever spoken.

29. There are times to be a parent and times to be a friend. Learn the difference.

30. Use "No" with great discrimination.

31. If you say "No" do it in a way that's not humiliating for the child.

32. Almost nothing is as important as it
     seems, and few things are important at
     all. Choose your battles with great care.

33. Watch closely. Changes occur every
     day.

34.   You will make mistakes. Learn from
        them.

35.   Allow your child to make mistakes. He,
        too, will learn.

36.   Do not force a child to eat anything.
      Hunger expresses itself in eating.

37.   Everything you say may return from
      your child to gladden or haunt you.

38.   Read to your child every day your child
      allows it.

39.   A baby cries not to irritate, but to communicate.

40.   If you do not let your child know you want to listen, she will stop talking to you.

41.   Give advice sparingly, and only after considerable thought.

42. A wise parent is often known by the things he or she does not say.

43. Punishment should fit the crime. If you administer punishment, first know assuredly what crime your child has committed.

44. Slapping or beating a child is not punishment. It is bullying at best, and physical abuse at worst.

45. It is natural for a child's attention to wander with great rapidity. It is the result of wonder.

46. If you have rules, you must also have reasons. Both you and your child need to know both.

47. Children want to know the rules.

48.   Conflict does not result from a lack of love, but failure to lovingly resolve conflict does.

49.   Having a pet can teach your child love and responsibility, but plan on cleaning out kitty's litter box often by yourself.

50.   Work diligently at being fair even though life isn't.

51. Do not place your child in the middle of an argument with your partner.

52. When your child is emotionally hurt, clean the wound before you apply a bandage.

53. The friends of your child should be as welcome in your home as your friends.

54.   Take family trips even if your child misses a few days of school.

55.   Few things bring a parent and child together more immediately than sleeping in a tent.

56.   Surprise your child with gifts from time to time just because you like him.

57. It's OK to tell your child when you're having a "bad day."

58. Every impatience you show at your child's questions will undermine her willingness to ask another.

59. The life most well-lived is built upon these three foundation stones: self-love, self-knowledge, self-discipline.

60. Everyone is innocent unless proven guilty…even your child.

61. You cannot "save" time. It passes relentlessly. But you can choose how yours will be spent. Choose wisely.

62. From time to time, take your child to work with you. They want to know what you do.

63. Just as you do, every child needs to dream.

64. Count it priceless when your child shares one of her dreams with you. Listen with your heart.

65. Just as you do, every child needs to have secrets.

66. Count it priceless when your child shares one of his secrets with you. Guard the confidence with diligence.

67. Your relationships with your children will bloom most brightly when they are planted in the rich soil of time spent together. Plan at least a few hours a month alone with each of your children.

68. If you fail to admit to your child when you are wrong, you will eventually destroy your credibility.

69. The job of a judge is to be judgmental.
     The job of a parent is to be sensitive
     and understanding.

70. It is easy to be judgmental. It is difficult
     to be sensitive and understanding.

71. It is far, far better to ask the best question than to give the best answer.

72. If a child figures it out himself, he will think even better the next time.

73. Step in when you are needed. Step aside when you are not.

74.   Do not set unreasonable standards.

75.   A child will eventually measure her worth by the standards you helped her establish for herself, not by your standards.

76. Do not ever try to persuade your child that he does not feel what he says he is feeling.

77. You can never know what your child is feeling…but you can try.

78. One of the greatest and most important challenges facing a parent is teaching a child how to deal with emotions.

79. Laps were created as seats for children, no matter how old they are.

80.   Bribery is not legal. It certainly has no place in the raising of a child...unless you're utterly desperate.

81.   Children learn to make decisions by making decisions. Let them.

82.   "A promise made is a debt unpaid."
      – Robert Service.

Keep your promises to your child.

83. A child will see things you've forgotten how to see. Pay attention.

84. They will have insightful opinions because they are children. Listen.

85. After watching a movie together, ask your child what he thought.

86. If you remove all the risks from a child's life, you will remove all the living from a child's life.

87. Teach them to prepare food. It will be messy, but it is important.

88. If you ask your child a question, wait for the answer.

89. Choose your words carefully. You can never "unsay" anything.

90. Do not ever finish a child's sentence for him.

91. The busier your life, the more critical it is to find time for your children.

92.   Anger may be appropriate. Thoughtless expression of anger is never appropriate.

93.   Do not let the sun set on your anger.

94.   If you can truly remember when you were your child's age, you are an astounding person. Use that knowledge wisely.

95. Rejoice when your children want to do things without you almost as much as you rejoice when they want to do things with you.

96. To act loving when you do not feel loving is not being a fraud. It is being a great parent.

97.   Your child will spend a lot of time
        trying to be like you. Spend time trying
        to be like your child.

98.   If you want everything to be perfect,
        you are doomed to be forever
        dissatisfied with your child.

99. Playing with your child is as important for you as it is for him.

100. Self-confidence grows from hearing positive words in response to actions.

101. A compliment is never wasted.

102. Find something about your child worthy of a compliment every day.

103. Spend at least a few minutes every day imagining the relationship you would like to have with your child.

104. If you are not spending time outdoors with them, you are severely limiting their growth and development.

105. If you hear yourself saying, "Because I said so!" you are hearing the wrong answer.

106. If you hear yourself saying, "Because I'm your mother!" your answer is just fine.

107. If you hear yourself saying, "Because I'm your parent, and we can discuss it when we get home!" that answer works, too.

108. Do not ask your child to do something
      you are not willing to do.

109. Complimenting your child to his face is
      not the same as bragging about your
      child to others. Do the first a lot and the
      second in great moderation.

110. To show an interest in your child's friends is to show an interest in your child.

111. If you want your child to brush his teeth, brush yours.

112. Yelling may be useful in getting a child's attention. After that, it is useless and destructive.

113. It's OK for your child to disagree with you. But it's not OK to leave the disagreement unresolved, even if you just resolve to disagree.

114. Tomorrow is forever to a child.
Rewards and punishments need to be
timely.

115. If you don't want a child to touch
something, keep it out of his reach.

116. A high IQ is not as important as a sense of humor. The first your child can do well without. The second is critical.

117. If you can't laugh at yourself, you don't have much of a sense of humor.

118. Children are not harmed by what their parents don't know, but by what their parents think they know that isn't true.

119. Experts who write books are people who make their guesses available to the public.

120. Read books on how to be a good parent. It won't hurt and it might help.

121. Do not make fun of what your child says to you unless you want him to stop talking altogether.

122. Know infant and child CPR.

123. Bullies make threats. Parents should not be bullies.

124. Most arguments between parents and children result not from personal differences but from age differences.

125. Ask your child, "What would you like to do tonight?"

126. Just because they are shorter doesn't mean you have the right to talk down to them.

127. The best preparation for tomorrow is celebration of today.

128. "Why?" is the most important question your child will ask.

129. Act, don't react.

130. Your child becomes trustworthy by being trusted.

131. Give your children enough time to be punctual.

132. Do unto others as you would have your child do unto others.

133. If you think you can discipline your child into being what you want, think again. What you can do is teach self-discipline.

134. Assumptions are the foundation of ruin. Gather information and make decisions.

135. If you don't want your child to get his clothes dirty, keep him naked.

136. Encourage your children to interact with other grown-ups.

137. Grandparents were created to spoil children. Let them.

138. Kindness is the act of treating people better than most of them deserve. The world cannot hold enough kindness. Teach your children well.

139. If your child does something helpful without being asked, be very sure to say thanks.

140. Fairy tales aren't just stories about fairies, but stories about good and bad, right and wrong, and life. So what if they're not politically correct.

141. No subject should be taboo when your child asks a question.

142. Everyone has the right to procrastinate from time to time, even children.

143. A child who is slow to respond is not the same as a child who is disobedient.

144. It's OK to ask your child "Why?"

145. Some of the values that you hold dear are not and may never be the values of your child.

146. Exercise daily. The benefits you receive will be passed on to your children.

147. How your friends and neighbors are raising their children is a poor guide for how you should raise yours.

148. Make sure your children know what to do in case of a fire.

149. At least once in your child's life, plant a garden, even if it's tiny, and tend it together, and watch things grow.

150. Meals are times for eating and peaceful conversation, not times for complaining and correcting.

151. Teach your children how to wash the dishes. The lessons they'll learn are more valuable than the glasses they'll break.

152. Fear is an unacceptable tool when used to motivate children.

153.   If you hear yourself saying, "This is
       going to hurt me more than it's going to
       hurt you," you're lying.

154.   Pain is as necessary a part of life as joy.

155.   Avoid being a source of pain whenever
       possible.

156. Practice what you preach. Even better, practice instead of preaching.

157. Sometimes doing too much for your child is as destructive than doing too little.

158. Nothing tells your child you care more than choosing to be with him.

159. It is not the responsibility of your child to fulfill your dreams.

160. If you want to have a sincere conversation with your child, arrange for your eyes to be on the same level with hers.

161. It is impossible to read the newspaper and answer your child's sincere question at the same time.

162. If your child does not learn to express his anger in healthy ways, it will build up inside him until he explodes.

163. Rules are easy to establish and difficult to maintain. Attitudes are difficult to establish and easy to maintain.

164. Some of the things in your child's life you'll want most to take charge of are none of your business.

165. To withhold the truth is not an act of kindness; it is an act of deception.

166. Honesty means telling the truth, but it does not mean telling everything you are thinking.

167. tact, n., 1: "a keen sense of what to do or say in order to maintain good relations with others or avoid offense," (Webster), 2: a necessary tool for anyone who wants to be a good parent.

168. Doing your very best is overrated. Often just doing something is more than enough.

169. In parenting there is very much art and very little science.

170. Remember: Smoking is unhealthy for you and your children.

171.   "Whoever has no patience has no wisdom."
       – Sa'di.

172.   You can change many of your child's shortcomings if you have a change of attitude.

173.   Politeness counts.

174. Don't embarrass your children in public. Use a code word to cue them about their inappropriate behavior.

175. Teach your children to feel their feelings and control their actions.

176. Teach your children to share. But remember sharing is a very confusing concept.

177. It's OK for your child to have "special possessions" all to himself.

178. You don't always have to make it better, but you can provide a lot of comfort by listening.

179. Many parents confuse unlimited attention with unlimited love. Sometimes it's more caring to take a break and get away from your children.

180. Encourage negotiation.

181. If you can combine discipline with respect, your child will learn to make his own decisions.

182. Remember that children are not always motivated by the same factors as adults.

183. Focus on the process, not the outcome.

184. Nurture your child's desire to learn by creating an environment where it can happen freely.

185. Schedule time to talk to your child every day.

186. Helping with daily "chores" builds competent people.

187. Who started it isn't important, how you resolve it, is.

188. You cannot make a child chew and swallow.

189. Don't confuse consistency with rigidity. Rules should be made of flexible material.

190. Dessert should not be a reward.

191. If there is no junk food in the house, children will seek eating alternatives.

192. Teaching your child to cope isn't the same as making it all better.

193. It's OK for your child to question the rules.

194. Say "Yes" often.

195. Let the consequences teach. Resist the urge to nag.

196. If you feel like saying "I told you so," the child already remembers.

197. Don't put too much stock in sitting still. It's overrated.

198. Know which decisions your child isn't ready to make.

199. Deal with childhood aggression calmly. Don't overreact…especially when your child does.

200. Be silly.

201. Accept your child's temperament… especially if it's unlike yours.

202. All healthy relationships require compromise.

203. Don't compromise on safety issues.

204. Ask your children how they feel.

205. Uphold family traditions.

206. Make up new traditions.

207. Blow up the TV.

208. Your presence helps build your child's confidence.

209. Children need to "fit in."

210. The shortest route to a child's heart starts from being there.

211. Relaxed parents tend to raise relaxed children.

212. Don't over-schedule your child's time. Freedom from rules and the chance to do as you choose is important.

213. A child can't handle having too much freedom and power. Provide limits and structure.

214. Don't be afraid to ask for help from someone you trust.

215. Don't worry. The things you waste the most time worrying about won't happen anyway.

216. Some of the things that bother you the most, such as his strong will, become some of the things most valuable to him later in life.

217. Remember "good" children sometimes make "bad" choices.

218. Children learn to whine. Be careful it's not you who taught them.

219. Sharing sadness is the beginning of healing.

220. Give your child a chance to entertain himself.

221. Encourage your child to spend time alone. It builds self-reliance and independence.

222. You can't buy happiness, even though it's fun to try.

223. Teach your child to wash his hands. He'll be sick less frequently…and he'll look better.

224. Do not teach your children to impress people. Teach them to live in a way that makes them happy.

225. Practice dealing with tough situations with your child. Role-play. Predictability will give them control in the future.

226. Great parents are people who consistently ask themselves if they're doing the job right. Poor parents don't think about it.

227. Kiss your child good night, every night.

228. If you aren't sure how to answer a child's question, begin by admitting it to the child.

229. The quickest way to get a child's cooperation is to ask for the child's help.

230. Encourage fantasy. It forms a foundation upon which a fantastic life can be built.

231. Your child's anger at you is also an expression of her trust in your love.

232. Children are loaned to you for safekeeping, not given into your care forever.

233. The only control your child can exercise over you is control you have given him.

234.   Try to remember those things your parents did that you promised yourself you would never do when you were a parent.

235. Your child will remember your tone of voice long after she has forgotten everything you said.

236. Unkind words not only wound your child's spirit but also teach her how to be unkind.

237.   Do not discourage your child's
       "helpfulness." It won't increase
       your efficiency now, but it will
       later. And more important, feeling
       helpful is a wonderful experience.

238. Go camping where you will contact absolutely nothing human other than yourselves.

239. Teach your children why and how to dial 9-1-1.

240. Lighten up. Do not take anything too seriously…especially yourself.

241. Do not buy anything that
requires ironing.

242. Put up a bird feeder.

243. Sometimes read or make up stories with your child the hero of the tale.

244. Talking comes first. Speaking correctly comes later. There ain't no hurry.

245. Put those little protective plugs in every electric outlet that tiny fingers can reach.

246. Check the house once again to make sure nothing poisonous is within reach.

247. It's OK to cry at the sad parts.

248. Music eases the stress and adds to the wonder of life.

249. Accept graciously the fact that most of the work will have to be done during nap times.

250. If your child is not seat-belted in, do not let the car move.

251. Her ability to understand what you say will far exceed her ability to talk.

252. "I did it because it was fun, and fun is good."
– Dr. Seuss.

253. If it's really his room, let him keep it the way he wants.

254. If you tell him it's "good for him,"
     you'll almost guarantee he won't like it.

255. Give an allowance because it teaches
     financial responsibility and not because
     you expect work in return.

256. Children are not servants. Children are not hired hands. If they have chores, it's because they're part of a family.

257. Just because you understand what that baby talk means doesn't mean you should talk that way too.

258. Don't ask to know anything you don't want to know.

259. Stop and look at every rainbow.

260. It's OK to sneak into his room at night to make sure he's still breathing.

261. Teach your children to recycle.

262. If the restaurant doesn't have a
      highchair, bring your own.

263. People who have no children
will think they know all about
raising yours.

264. Before taking another parent's advice, take a close look at her children.

265. If you hear another parent saying to you "Well, my parents did it, and it didn't hurt me…," ignore the advice.

266. If you lock your house, make sure you have a key secreted outside somewhere.

267. If you don't have two bathrooms, you'll wish you did.

268. Do not fail to appreciate any gift from your child.

269. Check the pockets before the clothes go into the washer.

270. Two of the first things your child should memorize are his street address and phone number.

271. Curiosity killed the cat. Your child is a human.

272.   Avoid sunburns.

273.   Don't take them to Toys R Us and not
       buy them anything. It's simply child
       torture.

274.   Don't take them to McDonalds and
       expect them to "eat first" while
       watching other children in the playland.
       More torture.

275. Sometimes let your children stay too long at the park.

276. The earth is their mother, too. Teach them to love her.

277. If there's any doubt about whether or not you should criticize your child, don't.

278. Defend a cause together.

279. Teach your child to pick up litter.

280. Occasionally free up some time for yourself by letting them watch The Lion King twice in a row.

281. Let your children mess up the house.
      Let them clean it up when they're
      finished.

282. Routines create apathy. Break out of the
      rut from time to time. Picnic on the
      porch. Camp in the living room.

283. "The bond that links your true family is not one of blood, but of respect and joy in each other's life."
– Richard Bach.

284. At least once a year watch How the Grinch Stole Christmas and The Lorax together. Make it a family tradition.

285. Don't expect teenagers to get excited about family vacations. It doesn't mean they're not.

286. Let them run wild outside, but set up boundaries so you'll know where to send the search party.

287. Teach your children what to do if they're lost.

288. Play in the rain.

289. Take your child to swimming lessons.

290. Allow your children the right to change their minds.

291. You can let your child get a weird haircut, but you don't have to pay for it.

292. Teach your children the difference between bickering and debating.

293. Remember a high energy level is a positive trait.

294. Take time to talk with your child's teachers.

295. Try to attend every event in which your child is a participant.

296. Intelligent and observant children try the patience of their parents the most.

297. Reward effort as well as achievement. Ice cream goes down just as smoothly when you lose the game.

298. When you've finished answering a question, stop talking.

299. Home school your child even though you send him to school every day.

300. Stand together with the wind in your faces.

301. Watch sunsets.

302. Teach your child how to use the library.

303. Remember bike helmets save lives.

304. Take a first aid course and keep a first aid kit handy.

305. Milestones to watch for because they come so quickly: first word, first steps, first sentence, first poop in the toilet, college graduation, marriage, the birth of your first grandchild.

306. Sick kids congregate at the doctor's office. Make sure your child is sick before you go.

307. Don't deny having an argument with your partner, but let the children know you worked it out.

308. Poopy happens.

309. Do not say derogatory things about your partner to your child.

310. It is an expression of power to forbid. It is an expression of love to allow. It is wisdom that knows which one to do.

311.   Love means being supportive of your children even when you are not supportive of their actions.

312.   Haste makes waste.

313.   As soon as they stop pulling on your leg and asking to be lifted up you'll wish they hadn't.

314. Unreasonable punishment teaches them to try harder to not get caught the next time.

315. A child who says "I hate you" has complete faith that you will keep loving her.

316. False praise devalues all praise.

317. empathy, n., "1: the action of understanding, being aware of, being sensitive to…" (Webster), 2: a critical element in good parenting.

318. To err is human, to forgive, a parental necessity.

319. They'll have to cry themselves to sleep a few nights before they learn about bedtime.

320. Track an animal in freshly fallen snow.

321. Parenting is half initiative and half knowing how to let things roll along on their own.

322. Here is a secret about being a great parent: Be in the Right Place at the Right Time.

323. Zoos were created for the child in all of us.

324. Do not rush a child into growing up. There's no advantage to being an adult.

325. What you put into loving your child is what you will get out.

326. The best way to eliminate worry is to do something.

327. Allow a child to cautiously examine any subject that arouses his curiosity.

328. Every once in a while, it's OK to skip school and go for a walk.

329. Encouragement is best expressed in compassion.

330. At least one reason for a tree is climbing it.

331. When you feel like you've reached the end of your endurance, it's time to conserve your energy.

332. Self-love and self-importance are radically different.

333. If it's not working for you and your child, stop doing it.

334. Self-sacrifice is not a virtue. You will not help your children by failing to take care of yourself.

335. You will teach your child
values whether you intend to
or not.

336. Emotions are not "good" or "bad." Emotions just are.

337. If you think you're right and everybody else thinks you're wrong, maybe you should reconsider.

338. Be careful who you have on the speed-dial buttons of your phone.

339. If you have a favorite child,
avoid any show of it.

340. Keep your child's vaccinations up to date.

341. Allow your child time to solve minor problems so he'll be able later to solve major ones. In other words, the round peg simply won't go in the square hole.

342. Your agenda will usually differ from theirs, but that doesn't mean yours is better.

343. "Please" and "Thank you" are still important.

344. No matter how expensive the toys you buy, he'll spend more time banging rocks around inside a tin can.

345. Keep reading aloud to your child long after she can read it herself.

346. It's OK to believe in Santa Claus, the Tooth Fairy and the Easter Bunny for as long as you can.

347. Teach them that their happiness does not depend on the opinions or actions of other people.

348. Showing them pictures of how dorky you looked in junior high school won't make them feel better.

349. If you have to read Green Eggs and Ham six times in a row, an aspirin helps.

350. They're supposed to get up early on Christmas morning.

351. Marvel at the magic!

352. Few children will fail to endure a hardship when they realize something better will be gained by it.

353. Tell them this until they understand: It is better to light one candle than curse the darkness.

354. His soul needs as much nourishing as his body.

355. No better food for the soul exists than the wild, untrammeled places of earth.

356. Climb a mountain.

357. Water made the Grand Canyon not because it fails to yield but because it relentlessly moves toward its goal.

358. All wisdom has one ultimate goal: self-sufficiency.

359. The world will be a better place, and they'll feel better about being a part of it, if they learn to bear the responsibility for their own actions.

360. Nothing in life is permanent

361. Just when he finally can give you a challenging game of chess, he leaves home.

362. If you have taught them how to learn,
     you have given them almost everything.

363. Celebrate the journey!

364. Finish what you start.

365. If you have taught them how to get along without you, you have prepared them for life.